ABOUT THE AUTHOR

Golnoosh Nour is a poet, prose writer, and lecturer. She's the author of *The Ministry of Guidance and other stories* – shortlisted for the Polari Prize 2021. Her work has also appeared in Granta, Spontaneous Poetics, and Columbia Journal amongst others. She has co-edited Magma 80 and an anthology of contemporary queer writing forthcoming from Muswell Press.

https://www.gnour.com
Twitter: @DrNourrr

Golnoosh Nour
ROCKSONG

VERVE
POETRY PRESS
BIRMINGHAM

PUBLISHED BY VERVE POETRY PRESS
https://vervepoetrypress.com
mail@vervepoetrypress.com

All rights reserved
© 2021 Golnoosh Nour

The right of Golnoosh Nour to be identified as author of this work has been asserted in accordance with section 77 of the Copyright, Designs and Patents Act 1988.

No part of this work may be reproduced, stored or transmitted in any form or by any means, graphic, electronic, recorded or mechanical, without the prior written permission of the publisher.

FIRST PUBLISHED OCT 2021

Printed and bound in the UK
by ImprintDigital, Exeter

ISBN: 978-1-912565-62-7

For anyone who gets it.

CONTENTS

BASS *(Songs of Home)*

Sculptures	13
The Wicked Capital	15
Mother Murder	17
Hiraeth	19
Sometimes Our Persona Melts in the Sun	20
My Mother Is My Lover	23
In Your Arms I Am A Boy	24
Through A Screen Darkly	25
Cat Worship	27

VOCALS *(Songs of Desire)*

Dream	31
Psychosis	32
The Leather Sun	33
Game	34
introvert schizo is a #mood or Cheap Plastic Thoughts	36
Cut-up Boy	38
Lovesong	40
Bastard	41
Made Up	43
Attitude	45
Hologram	46

Boy Museum	47
Lost Cult	49
Eye of the Storm	51

DRUMS *(Songs of Selves)*

Ode to Self	55
A Peacock Is a Poem	56
Infected Parrot	58
Texting the Teenage Self	60
The Cruelty of Impatience	62
I Am Ash on Wednesdays	63
Euston Station	65
Cliff Trip	66
Ritual	68
Blood Days	69
Bad News	70
This Is A Painting Called Motherhood	74
Sunlit Suicide in the Bathtub	75
Smoke Sky	77
RAGESONG	78
A Manifesto: The Future Is Queer	80

Acknowledgements

ROCKSONG

BASS
(Songs of Home)

Sculptures

but why do I have to explain.
why can't I just wear
my blue lipstick and be *ironic*
artsy and *eccentric*. why do
I have to remind them what they've
done to my land, or why sanctions
are bad. why do I have to
be the teacher rising from the grave
of Politics. why should I be the one shouting
we need transgression, darling, not progression
as though I were the chosen one
why did I consume my youth in
sad universities to confirm what I knew
all along. to tediously intellectualise
my instinct – when I could have spent
this time burning a bank, or a church, or even a mosque
where dollar prays that queers will die.
why do I have to explain
why a lunar boy in a dress who murmurs
my art hardens his nipples makes my cunt
jump. why do I have to justify?
why can't I just open
The Picture of Dorian Gray, page 155
'To define is to limit.'
and just stare as though I am gazing at
Basil's painting – but instead
I am the one ageing. why do I have to inform
my father of my sex life when my mother
the sculptor, carved my flesh for years
so I'd be as cultured as her dusty library, but she made
me a bruised slut. why did I desire her
dead like the ultimate Freudian cliché so

I could have my father to myself. but now
that she's gone, my father and I
are still apart, cutting each other, yielding blood
and we both think the fox that visits
my girlfriend's garden is my mother.

The Wicked Capital

Tehran means reading never-ending Russian novels under my duvet,
glitterless gay parties until the morning Azan, until the birds scream,
mahogany cafés serving cinnamon tea and vanilla I scream,
Tehran is smoke and fury. It is fuming.
Tehran is static traffic, it is also fenugreek,
all-girl schools, all-boy love, and compulsory hijab,
and the evergreen Shahid Beheshti University where we exchanged
gay kisses but gay did not mean happy, it meant
homo whore harassed faggot corrupt beautiful.
The university whose rules we shattered in our attempts to
become Lord Byron. A garden that is still shining, a neon
green sun in the north west of Tehran that inhaled our ashes, while we
smoked our youth and spat colonial classics, empowering ourselves.

(Now the question is: Will we ever be truly empowered? We,
the despondent snobs from the top universities of Iran, who ended up in
    the bottom
universities of Brexitland, Dumpland, The North Pole, doing degree after
degree after degree so we/they can forget our skin colour and forgive
our accent even though we are pale like flour, and quiet
like infected parrots, will we ever be empowered?)

In Tehran we are still powerless, even though
it is officially our homeland: our sealess port.
Tehran, the harbour of pollution where fast cars screech
American pop in ambivalent alleyways paved with martyrs' blood.
I have never seen a city capable of containing so much love and hate.

Tehran is my parents and our house,
my siblings and my best friend, his passion
for beautiful boys and avant-garde theatre, and the scenario
of our eternal escape. Tehran is my grandmother,

cherry pickles that she made just for me with specifically
rotten sour cherries that surprisingly tasted like god,
her God, that was not my god, and became a gap that devoured our love.
Tehran is my real room, my bookshelf, my vanity table, crowded
with bottles of blue varnish – my first rainbow flag.
Tehran is aromatic; herbs, saffron, dried lime,
turmeric, salt, bloody beans, red meat, brown flesh.
After Persian cuisine, nothing tastes great.

Tehran is Arabic prayers and Persian poetry:
Bookshops floating in the sizzling summer streets:
Forough Farrokhzad, Sohrab Sepehri, and Sadegh Hedayat, but also
preposterous books such as bad translations of
American self-help and Mein Kampf.
Everything for a cheap price! And the everlasting question:
How can this country survive when Hedayat
killed himself and Forough died at such a young age?

Tehran is fear. More wars, more sanctions, more inflation.
The morality police. Our government, the US government, Saudi Arabia,
and the government of Israel. Fear of all the governments, and fear of
    more chaos.
Fear of expenses. Fear of being stuck. Fear of leaving. And of returning.
Fear of missing. Fear of losing and fear of winning.
Fear of anarchy, and love of anarchy.
And love.

Living in Tehran is like being in love with the villain
everyone judges and wonders why, but one will not
lower oneself to explain the attraction.
The moment anything is justified, it becomes boring, common, worldly.
This is why when people ask where in Iran I am from,
I respond, *the wicked capital,*
saturated with gold oil, dripping with black glory,
come in but stay out, so you won't regret it.

Mother Murder

The Bitch is dead. Bitch as in God. God as in commander, as in ruler, as in our beloved dictator, our faithful mother, snobbish scholar, mesmeric philosopher, generous professor, socialist empress, enthusiastic God–worshipper, God–weaponiser, successful cigarette–quitter, beautiful fighter, the taunting Goddess of I'm the best, fuck the rest, you do as I say as I rule my rule is the rule of God and the law of intelligence. The pedantic Michael Jackson-loving queen of I'm too cultured for pop culture. A charismatic chasm of lethal words and killer looks, the assassin, but not the assassinated.

And it was March, March, March that turned out to be the cruellest month. March that murdered her. In the blossom, her death bloomed, it boomed – an explosion even louder than her birth. By April we were all insane, crawling inside our murderous motherland, lost in its smoky cemetery, dragged towards her grave, drugged by pain, we screamed our tears as madness does. In disbelief, in sorrow, in shame.

Then galloped back to nonchalant Europe, seeking the nonexistent cure.
How is it possible? Even after years.
How could it be her of all the people who could have been taken away?
The ever–tormenting question: Why her?

O Mother,
What have I left out?
What have I forgotten?
I should have done something to keep you safe from Death.
O Mother, since your demise,
regret became a rope around my throat.
You were my safety net, even though at times, you were a pair of golden eyes that radiated murder.
Why did you have to stretch out your smooth claws to Death?
Can I blame you? Why do I blame myself?

And how can we survive this symphony of sorrow when even your resentful colleagues say the university is empty without you?
How are we supposed to respond? Our lives are emptied.
What are we supposed to say to our father, a mountain flower that's been severed from his mountain?

Farewell to you, Mother:
To your thunderstorms of Islamic Socialism
To your curled Persian mouth, which you painted with Chanel
To your intellectual patriotism
To your beatific lack of shame
To your full lips of *Falsafeh*
To you, the kindly jackal of The University
To you, the life-giver, the murderer, The Universe.

Hiraeth

One silver day my father called from the North of Iran,
I could hear the sea in his voice and the sun
dangling from the ceiling of his worn villa; my skin
streaming to the source of his humid voice,
I feigned love for London, this gilded well
I, an ambivalent immigrant, always on time for visa stamps,
vomiting smiles at the police, concealing
my stress, sticking to deadlines like they are guns,
thrilled to be tolerated by whiteness, the sparkling promise
of praise. Speaking my second language
like chewing ice: foreign words swimming in my foreign mouth
tricky, always surprising – a secret I shouted to
betray a friend, but then I recalled
I have been to many a house, alas, never a home
and I betrayed myself by confessing to my father:

I want to be where you are
melting in the Caspian under its ruthless sun
until my pale skin turns brown
and I become a real brown person who
can keep secrets and admits that she misses
the streets of her burning country

Sometimes Our Persona Melts in the Sun

You and I talk about how your wife tortures your son,
then you cry, dropping your head on my shoulder, and mumble, 'I'm tired.'
I try my best to sip my ice tea, bewildered and paralysed.

You and I talk about how we should only seduce stunning guys,
endorphin wraps around our throats - choking us,
my hands are sweaty, hence I'm ashamed.

You say you would lick my sweat if it weren't for the eyes
around us in the café, on the streets, in our rooms, on our walls,
the petty gods, eternally bored, praying

we would cross the line, so they could punish us some more.
You and I always in the garden of our far away café
We have no house we are not homeless, just unhomed,

sharing houses with people we don't know:
our parents, our teachers, our partners, our prophets,
our boundaries, our Imams, our bad luck.

You and I have always talked about
Oscar Wilde and Ahmad Shamloo, about Forough Farrokhzad
We have always lost.

You crave to be the devil, but I know you are just a weeping saint.
I want to look at you when you talk. And when you don't talk
when you play with your summery, little son

even when you argue with your falling wife
who knows your so-called secret. Why shouldn't she argue?
Why shouldn't she threaten you?

Why shouldn't she abuse your son to make up
for all the times you kissed men behind her back?
For every time you told me I am your love, your only friend, your confidant.

Do you think she's wary of my strange existence?
'That annoying little girl, so full of herself.
Why are you friends anyway?'

Our little gods judge us and we fail and we break and we fall,
but you lift me up, and I pick you up among negative HIV tests,
and hedonistic jokes,

we are always scared of our final punishment:
STDs, execution, shame, exile, forced suicide, what is it?
Give it to us already.

You and I, the dark lesson for the future nation
so they will always obey, they will always buy lies.
We are also frightened of being found out that we are not evil

that we cry in the dark, and laugh in the light
that your fast car is just a façade of your suicide
we get drunk on Aragh and we look as though we want to fuck all the pretty boys.

We are here for the sake of fuck; that is the plan, the plot, our persona
whereas we only want to bang our heads against
the sharp edges of the festive table and die

or not die, maybe survive, perhaps spend some time in a silver hospital
where nurses are non-judgmental –
they'll even sleep with us if we ask them with some charm

where you're not married, and I'm not stuck
where it is raining, and this aggressive sun is gone.
Now, I am standing in the dark.

I lost my sight in the constant presence of the sun which
has always been too bright for my eyes.
My weak eyes. My wicked eyes.

I know you are standing somewhere near me,
as blind and as lost as me, hoping you will drown soon
in a rainy sea where there is no sun, but your son,

no god, apart from our love.
I can feel you're breathing near me, you are almost living

Tell me where you are.

My Mother Is My Lover

I'm so imperious I could be the sun, but
I'm only the son of a smuggled sunflower, and my
fear of loss. Paralysis dominates and I think I am done
palpitating. The despondent prince of the furious valley
of sex. But today is heaven I'm Daddy's perfect girl.
When I tell him I'm tired, he snickers,
'But look at your beautiful face!'
I glance at my sallow countenance and swallow my tears.
We stare into our screens, send pixelated kisses, and
I feel like a failed piece of art, an orphaned desire.
At thirty-one I still want to be Daddy's little girl
like when I was eight and came second in a math test.
I was over the sun until father said,
second is great, but you could've been first.
He teases my brother, *You need to learn from her!*
She always had it in her!
and flashes me his artificial teeth.
My brother giggles but narrows his eyes. I smile it off as if
Mother were rampaging again.
I have won a few wars but do not feel like
the victor my father raised and my mother despised.

Two hours later, I'm spread on a sinking sofa
listening to my lover call me a 'narcissist' for the twenty ninth time
I produce the fur scarf she knitted for my birthday –
a gold fox, wrapping around my throat, tighter
by the second. She is screaming for me to stop.
I feel my intestines escaping my throat,
when I taste her tears, I let go.

Maybe it is true what they say:
In the end, every boy marries his mother.

In Your Arms I Am A Boy

A sparrow, trapped and warmed in your hands,
a nightingale singing the songs of misery and victory,
a boy who competes with other boys to win at pool, at fights, at life.
A boy who murmurs in your ears that you are an empress for whom
he is ready to murder everyone else.

A jealous boy, a delicate boy, a delicious boy.
An inebriated boy, a pauper, a landless poet, a nomad who
has been accused of being a solipsistic prince.
A socialist boy, a sociable boy, an isolated boy, an island in love
with the ocean that is drowning it.

A brown boy, daggered by injustice,
an attacked prince like Siyavash, dragged
to walk through flames to prove his innocence.
As I storm through the fire, you hold my hands
like a bouquet of blossoming roses.

You are right, my empress, I am nothing but a wounded prince:
stabbed in the back and front by all my friends and
none of my enemies, bleeding on your cold marble, and you,
mesmerised by my golden blood,
will betray the world to save your boy.

Through A Screen Darkly

What is it that my brother and I share?
It is more than blood & flesh.

He writes in a river of Persian, I swim in a sewer of English. My
every word a failed labour, a treacherous stench, a lexical accident.

My English is shit just like my Farsi. I admit to him. He nods.
He gets it. We've lost our tongues, our mother, our safety, still

we revel in incestuous uncertainty. We share siblings, a bed
when possible. We hold each other through our obsessions:

lip balm, gossip, sunflower seeds, pretentious cinema,
obscure songs on Spotify, teenage memes, & worst of all:

We joke about betrayal; we blame everyone: *we had bad
role models, our relatives, our favourite artists, they did us harm*

Bergman and his divorces... I look at my brother through our
screens, he watches me watch him feed his cat half his steak.

She is conspicuously Persian, with an air of arrogance and
trauma, just like my brother, and perhaps like me.

Come to me, I tell him by saying your cat is gorgeously
possessive. I won't leave this country. My brother states, seemingly

not in response to me, but as a stubborn solution to the dilemma
of identity. Stay there – as long as you're happy.

Everywhere is dreary. I say, aware I make no sense.
How can I be sage when I am as lost as him, only in another place?

What is it that makes us close even when we are continents apart?
Even when he counts his calories & I eat and eat until I can't breathe

when he is tall & tanned, and I short & pale?
– a melting snowman, a withering carrot protruding from my face –

What is it that one scorching summer made
one of his lovers stare at us in furious disbelief, spitting

you look alike
you write alike
& you both cheat
why are you like this?

Cat Worship

A beautiful woman has a curtain of flesh. - Persian proverb

You & I are two fat cats in love
two voluptuous women
perhaps obese by cinematic standards
'unhealthy' by our mothers' concerns
only fleshy according to friends.
I cannot imagine myself alive
without your curtain of flesh.
I hide behind it like a shy child when
the world shouts at me, I shelter in your flesh
from pretty much everyone else:
the rich, them straights & the police
I too am a fat feline, terrified & disgusted by pigs.

You walk like a kindly matriarch, no trace of
hesitance in your small feet
your strength knows no shame
your long lashes are thorns in the eyes of envy
your crown of hair shines in the sun & rain
your power bejewelled by compassion
you cleanse the air with your soft breath
you beautify the sunlight with your manicured claws
you wave your scarlet nails in the air like a disdainful
diva, when I'm upset by pettiness, when I'm bruised & sick
paranoid — for the right reasons – at times even insane,
my only cure to be as close as possible:
warm velvet, my beatific shelter,
the only promise I cannot break.

VOCALS
(Songs of Desire)

Dream

Even though I do not think I think of her, she comes to me in a dream, murmuring

In another time, we'd be inside each other
All
The
Fucking
Time

Psychosis

my fingers press around your throat. your cock gets hard. I have been hard for you, for months. we have dreamed of this so many times we can't believe it's happening now. we are two boys together, giggling and teenaged, two women, raging and throbbing. whatever this is, it is not heterosexual. why can't I just shut up and not intellectualise. why can't I accept my clit trembles every time my sinful eyes fall upon a beautiful boy, like you. you, who could be anyone, and I am never satisfied; greed is my oxygen and I feel sick with desire and outrage all the time. and when I visit the doctors, I pray they prescribe suicide, boys, guns, and other drugs but they don't know anything. I don't need therapy. I need to scream and scratch myself and your skin, oh your soft skin that melts under my tongue as you beg me not to ever stop. this must be self-murder as I feel dead afterwards; this is not euphoria, darling, I am psychotic. I don't even know what I'm doing I am tired of being in love with my mother. I am tired of her undying death. I am tired of the illness she concealed. I am tired of her divine disapproval. I am tired of the family she left behind. I am sick of being loved, looked after, scarred, and trodden upon. you, mysterious passerby, delicate, porcelain boy dragging a suitcase exploding with scandal and drama, stroking my skin with your lithe fingers, you let me enter you, you don't get it but you do, it's all in the eyes and the fist and the betrayals and our sexy traumas. it's all in our scandalised bodies. you slut, why are you prettier than me, I ask you joyously, jealously, impulsively. you chuckle, you are so certain of your physicality that you know your strongest moments are when you lick your words and look directly into the sun as if it belongs to you. and maybe it does. it never belonged to me and it never will and it's true I even resent the sky. I want to pollute both of you and be calm.

The Leather Sun

It is five a.m. and there is a woman growing
inside my head. Not like a tumour –
but a flower that feeds on power
she makes me tremble.

Words devour me. I open my mouth
thirsty for more, this is a sweet-tasting storm
I know someday this bed of hers
will be my comfortable tomb.

For now, this monstrous bed is a gilded ship,
a surreptitious ship, my shelter,
I stare into her eyes until they are the sun and
I melt, melt, melt. It is true:

I am like Icarus in my ridiculous ambition and lack of abstinence
in my love of flight, height, and light,
but she calls me Napoleon, and
laughs in my ears [a choking sound]

her leather scent fills my throbbing nostrils like cocaine,
she kisses my neck and worships my shamelessness, she says
I am arrogant and licks my lips. Outside, the sun,
a blood red orange, waiting to be peeled by us.

Game

Level One: Bodies

I have fucked them all.
Them, the pretty men who walk in beauty
walk in my head, night and day, they stroll the restless
streets of my intoxicated psyche
waving their tight bums from left to right
like a bunch of royal cats.

Their cheekbones are my mountains of joy, which I ascend
until I reach the peak of their beauty
and my game until
I'm bored, bored
bored.

As soon as the sun starts melting in their eyes
I leave
I leave them
                          howling
falling
                  begging
by   my bed.

You have to vanish, like all surreptitious lovers
my beautiful boys
I have to go although the sun is melting in your eyes
و خورشید در چشمان شما ذوب میشود
and your necks are saplings in the dark.
و گردن شما نهالیست درخشان در باغی تاریک

Level Two: Nationalities

I am dark
and my mind is black
but my privilege isn't white
it is mad. My madness is my privilege,
this is how I shall mistreat you behind my mask of lunacy
made of logic and repression.

This is what happens:
At the end of the day, you sell your intelligence to the system and
purchase some madness to put on your face
like expensive make-up, it justifies all your wrongs
and in the morning, you spread my madness on your toast and bread
and digest it with tea.

(Interesting fact: we, Iranians, don't pour milk in our tea
this is our privilege.
Milkless tea
Dark tea
Black tea)

Level Three: Stage Four

Oh, my shiny darlings,
once you drink my frenzy, and my cloudy tea in my sunny country
once you worship my shark teeth, you become
just like me:

invincible and incurable
like stage 4 cancer

introvert schizo is a #mood or Cheap Plastic Thoughts

there are things beneath you, a cheap plastic table, an unmade bed
viral thoughts that spread in your blood, like wine, drugs, and #mood, cheap
things you feel but cannot claim: shameless shame, your filtered life on Insta,
your girlfriend fancying your best friend, your desire to beat up both of them,
your dead mother's sex life, your urge to fuck
a random boy on public transport, dominating
his delicate bones with your thumping cunt, these thoughts are all
beneath you. behave! you're sort of educated and somehow privileged
lucky, even #blessed, visceral violence is beneath you, useless
degrees in useless subjects, art and literature, ephemeral
friendships, tedious romances, are not beneath you, books
that no one else reads have been written for you, carbs
are beneath you, being vile and drunk is beneath you, smile! *you have everything!*
your girlfriend screams and everybody else agrees. this weirdness whatever it is
is beneath you. why do you have to ruin everything for cheap feelings that are
    beneath you?
there are things you're not allowed to articulate: your sympathies
for convicts, communists, dictators, your nostalgia for libertine cities
that don't exist embarrassing appetite for pop music for
hierarchical power are all beneath you, jealousy
is beneath you, it's a distant town in a country you're not allowed to love,
but you're social-media sexy, be happy, wanting
to be worshipped is a cheap plastic table, legs up in the air, piercing your skin,
    an ugly
dagger your sexual attraction to your sibling is
beneath you, your lack of faith in anything other than your ego
your feigned intellect, your paranoia
that you parade as passion, this paranoia, this poem
is beneath you, holding you like a cheap plastic seat with wobbly feet.

you swing your cold legs in the summer air, pretending
to enjoy the heat even though your specific skin can only feel cold and no heat,
you pretend to sweat, to wear a little black dress, to celebrate, you listen, this is just
another random party, but it hurts like a terrible poem, just another social
    commitment
to abhor and attend, and you water your tree with alcohol and convince
yourself you sound sane and it's okay that all your interesting conversations
happen inside your head; times like these close your eyes and guide
yourself to an empty bathroom, fist the mirror like it's a blond
boy on public transport,
then slit your wrists
#bleed

Cut-up Boy [1]

I've spent my life as a str8 boy
a shy boy
a submissive boy
holiday in Thailand with family
                                                a bored twink
Vodka, dogs, and folklore
still bored
I need   a pyscho perv, a sadistic str8 man, a cop, a criminal
to tie me up
                                        bruise me
beat me up
        electrocute the inside of my hole
I want to go naked into an abandoned barn
I am a sick animal; I want to be completely insane
I'm shaved oiled up trussed up and seasoned
                              a hard apple stuffed in my mouth
A construct of an encounter
Anal destruction
For I know   in carnage, I bloom, like a flower in dawn.

My turn ons are everything   extreme
execution, Tabasco sauce on my cock & balls, wedding rings.
I'll be ur carpet, ur furniture, ur seat
                              Frisk me, smoke me out
Bruise me, choke me with ur mind.
I want to talk about art, I want to be smart
but I don't know how, I'm too
pretty for anything but sex and I
hate it but I love it
My intentional madness is both Dadaistic and sexy

---

[1] All the lines of this poem – apart from one – have been lifted from Dennis Cooper's blog.

I want to be a character in transgressive lit and
be abhorred, adored, and pitied:
Sade, Delany, Cooper, Crowley, you name it and I
know it but I won't say it because
I am that pretty. And I might be
a maso trash, the shyest boy in class, but
U are not a Sir either,   u filthy pig
Nor are u my 'master',   u ugly shit!

To dominate me, u have to be better
than me. But how can anyone be
possibly superior
to me?

                        I am ready for all atrocities.

Lovesong

Impossible to express my feelings by just screaming
into an endless well, "I love you"
because it would be an attempt
to hold a mountain on a teaspoon.

You let me melt into you every dawn, and
every dusk, you let me chain you with the flesh of my lust.
You lie beside me like an orchid-shaped volcano,
exuding lava, because neither of us can be pleased by
anything less than conflagration.
We set ablaze every garden we have ever entered.

You unshackle and shackle me at the same time.
All with your eyes.
When, over petty matters, our impatient mouths burst with the blood of insults,
I escape from you to you.
You shelter in my trembling arms, and I in yours
and the fight becomes just another flight.

I wonder if we only get enraged so we can destroy each other better
in bed, your cold lips heat up as they hit mine,
two tigers roaming freely
but never free of each other, furiously in love,
we fight and reconcile and burn
the jungle with our branded tongues.

Bastard

I forgot about him until he came to me in a dream:
on a hazy beach in a blue bikini, his lips, plump and crimson.
The first time I met him, I was a dizzy virgin, eighteen,
and all I wanted was to be admired
by an older lecturer who looked as young as me.
Years later, in another country,
far from our flames, he comes back to me in a bikini, in blood lipstick
not saying anything, just gazing, small eyes squinting
from behind enormous glasses,
the eternal barrier between his skin and mine.
He always wore boring clothes, black and mustard yellow
but my dream queered him.
Did he ever want me? Sniffing my sour perfume in his sunlit office, he did
not touch me. His elegant hands, my ivory plants
caressed against my fingers twice, exchanging
Coetzee's *Disgrace*. Later he texted me in English
keep it as a present felt like an insult between my teenage legs
I assumed he did not want to end up like that professor
who was obsessed with Byron and slept with his student,
and subsequently was fired and his daughter got raped.
But my love was in love with linguistics.
He did not sleep with me
he deconstructed deconstruction so much so
that even I got bored
I opened my legs beneath my black hijab
convinced that he could see everything, and nobody
else could see anything. At the age of eighteen one is
convinced one can drink anything one desires,
even if that desire is married with two kids.
But I did not want to be fucked. And neither did he.
What were our nervous surreptions about?

Twelve years later:
As I sit behind my teacherly desk
discussing deconstruction,
I find myself mimicking him.
And in my dream, I have an epiphany:
I never desired him. I desired to *be* him. To shield behind
a desk, skimming students like a cat staring
at rats, and spitting, 'Foucault says every piece of art is a
bastard.'

Made Up

He smokes weed, more and more, leftover from last night and the day before,
revelling in the thought of the lies to his mother about quitting,
relishing the look of disbelief on her foundationed face.

Her foundation is soft and smells like a damp garden.
The boy looks in the mirror and
blushes.

He wears his 17-year-old innocence on his face over the powder.
On his bones, there is a dress
as pink as the orgasmic embarrassment on his cheeks.

His dark locks, a chaotic black river
on his pale face.
His naked feet fidgeting in the sunlight pouring from the ajar window.

This is an old English town where the sun
is the only gift
to be treasured.

And his mother who teaches history at school
to boys and girls like him and to black and immigrant kids, too
will be home soon.

He drinks his sizzling soup
and licks his lips clean from its orange red drops
then brushes his teeth with his mother's perfume.

He has never been so pleased with his father's death.
A dull professor. Sexless too – according to his mother.
His heart is a flying stone, too heavy and dynamic to wait.

He washes the dirty dishes to kill the thirsty seconds
then rinses his delicate hands beneath hot water
his skin burns like the thought of sin.

He stares at his mother's soup, slowly boiling
– a dark secret about to burst open, a delicious wound.
She is always hungry after school.

He looks in the mirror and blushes,
stroking his soft lips with his mother's pink lipstick, and suddenly
the door opens.

His mother is back at last.
Gazing at his image in the mirror, her blue eyes are beads of ice.
Her bag, matte black leather, a true animal rights activist's bag.

Her boy pulls up his frilly pink skirt, offering his toned white bum,
      pleading with her:
'Fuck me, mummy.
Hard.'

Attitude

Neon blue toe nails on pale feet
dead fish in a dried lake
pants pulled down, top pulled up
V is on.

Push your lovers under the carpet, instead of drugs,
sniff their ashes to stay healthy and ecstatic.
Dig a grave for expired blunders.
Victory is on its way,

inhale it like you inhaled boys in the rain.
V is calling you like roaring tigers in gilded forests and
withered flowers on your dusty windowpanes
when you were a virgin.

Hologram

I am in my blackest mood, and she
lies on the whiteness of my sheets in her
blackest bra, staring at the air I am supposed
to breathe, except that I cannot breathe.

Her black jeans are as tight as my lungs
I have coughed and fought all my sable life
My visions of her have become holographic bars behind which
I am trapped.

Like every melancholic captive, I love my dungeon
Like every claustrophobic patient, I loathe it
at times, I crave escape, but when she turns her pensive
head towards me, the darkness of her eyes hit mine, I

collapse to my knees, pulverised by her silver thunder.
Upon being touched by her flame fingers, and tongues of fire,
I explode. She celebrates my combustion by collecting my ashes
from her cool ceramic floor, warming them in her powerful grip

before sniffing me away. Later on, in a sunny concert hall,
she will lie to her envious friends, saying it was just cocaine.
I know I am her drug and it's what I have wanted to become
since I was a child.

Boy Museum

I cannot turn my head
cause this will be my death
an electric boy is sitting there
'there' becomes my direction
the destination of my head, hung
like a sad penis

I thirst because
boys are accessible
disposable
violently tender
their bodies swirl to suit me like a dress
twirl to wear me like my blazer

but I kick them away – it's unsafe, as though
safety ever matters, as if safety ever existed
I make myself tremble with laughter in
my swan bed until I can't breathe
and boys drip from my sheets
cause darling, we live the dream

We choke [on] boys
we smoke boys and become consumed
by their diaphanous image, the beauteous mirage
the soft warmth of their mouths
their restless elegance

Boys become birds I kiss with my arrows
boys become rays I kill with my jokes
boys become toys I throw in my storms
their scent is thunderous
so strong we suffocate
so mad we cackle.

And boys drip from my ceiling
onto my plate
I have nothing to bury
Mother warns *if you become a man-eater*
you'll betray your beloved.
But I've been betraying myself ever since I can remember.

Lost Cult

Lingering like smoke, I end
up in a broken park. Colourful flowers
scattered, like the toys of a mad toddler,
a bright curse that stalks my skin.

A poet murmurs, 'It is desire that
makes you follow someone in
the dark, to paths untrodden.'
And I have an epiphany;

A long time ago, she followed me
down a leafy corridor; two women
exuding Eros but heading nowhere;
how could the innocent me accept

that the person I desired the most,
desired me also? O she whom I
worshipped. She who would've killed
me, drinking my cunt.

Eye of the Storm

Everything is dark
apart from the lightning in the sky that pours
into our space. I lie on my belly on your bed
as you stand by the window wowing at the thunder
and I'm even jealous of the sky.
A woman we both admire asked me once, *why
do you always write about blood?*

And today was like any other day, we
hurt each other and healed each other
as though to have an excuse
to apologise, to declare
our love. This is not bdsm – there is no safe word,
no shiny pvc, no lightning whip, it has no tedious formula
it's not dirty, it is filthy; it is love.

We ate olives and almonds, watched
a sapphic film with a sad ending, painted our nails
neon green, and listened to the rain, and I recalled a dead friend
who said, *nobody howls like Heathcliff from love, it would be
hilarious in the age of Tinder*, and maybe I'm in agreement, but not today.
You open the window to the dark rain, and as the electricity
slaughters the sky, you howl and I notice I've never been so calm.

DRUMS
(Songs of Selves)

Ode to Self

'We survived and survival breeds desire for more self.' – Audre Lorde

I am that
the fatigued knight wading through the morning light
like Moses gaping the Nile

I am that
the black rose in winter, dead
butterflies dripping from my bruised petals.

I am it
The 'it factor', the cool factor minus, the cold factor plus, the hot
mess, the browned flesh, the queer crushed
by Authority, forever refusing to agree with anything
other than my own elegant violence, my
autumnal tendencies that I catch in the river of my mirror – the only
    truth teller

for I am that,
the breathing painting in the attic
the 'darling' collector
the cold sore in summer
the sore throat in spring
the allergy screeching at the skin.

I am it
the blue silk with a scarlet kernel,
wrapped in my gold cape, embroidered by thorns, I pounce
over the fence into the abyss to caress
my horns, and to plant myself in fertile soil, roots hard in the ground;
shaking off tornados from my trembling naked branches, I grow tall,
old, skyward, enamoured, pure.

A Peacock Is a Poem

After Aubrey Beardsley

A silver platter embroidered with gold
ashes. A poem is not a poem if it doesn't
weep gilded decadence. A poem is not a poem
if it doesn't look like a slender boy in a peacock
skirt. It is not a poem if the boy does not claim
to be Venus. It is not a poem if Venus does not
stay awake until dawn, coiffing her hair. It is not a
poem if Venus does not behead religion.
It is a ballad when religion bleeds obsidian stones
It is an epic when religion apologises and Venus
spanks it with her diamond whip. Religion writhes in blood,
asking for more. But our boy, Venus gets bored.
She takes off her peacock skirt, displaying her crystal
penis. Religion gets aroused, excited even, but Venus
throws his severed head in her golden bin, alongside a few saints
and prophets, who are all pleading, bleeding, in vain.
A poem is only a poem if it's a naked woman seeking
Lovers. A poem is only a poem if it's a many breasted dragon
Her breasts covered with crimson damask, and strewn with
gay flowers; irises, columbines, carnations.
A poem is only a poem if it's a decadent diamond
It is not a poem if it doesn't wear a peacock skirt
It is not a poem if it does not display a silver tray of sex and the grotesque.
A poem is not a poem if it doesn't destroy itself.
A poem is only a poem if it's an ivory piece
A poem is not a poem if it doesn't tease with the memory of a grotesque
dream – or a charming nightmare.
A poem is not a poem if it's not a curious tale.
A poem is a sonnet if it crushes iambic pentameters.
A poem is an elegy if it celebrates decadence
It is a sestina if it knows the dance of the seven veils

It is an ode if it mocks its object of desire.
A poem is a poem if it writes letters to its critics patronising them to tears.
A poem is only a poem if it escapes the injustice of juries and
the shuffling of dealers. A poem is not a poem if it claims
Shakespeare for its favourite poet, Beethoven for its favourite
composer, and Raphael for its favourite painter.
A poem is only a poem if it doesn't confess.
A poem is a true poem if it's a mad woman beheading prophets.
A poem is a poem if it's a valiant warrior, wrapped
in peacock feathers.

Infected Parrot

I have no place to stay.
My bed is overflowing with boys,
my mind with girls.
Gender is a performance
I repeat, like an infected parrot.

I am an eternally inebriated animal,
hence my bed is hollow, my mind an asylum
filled with refugees who will be deported
back, back, back.
To war.

But we have no place to go.
My bed is broken and
even though my mind is blooming
like a European Museum of Contemporary Art
I know I cannot stay.

I do not know about the refugees,
I am an international student,
paying, not to be a threat
to national security.
Look at my exotic feathers.

I am an international parrot,
my bed is filled with dysfunctional languages
with German philosophy, British fiction, and Persian poetry
with murderous grammar rules
with alcoholic European dreams.

I learn things, and repeat them until
my beak bleeds,
And I write with my blood
poems about painless pleasure.
And I shall always lie and repeat:

I am not political. I am a woman of pleasure,
a cold lake full of colourful shells.
I'm not wounded I'm not bothered by the bloodshed
by the crushing cages of the mad Middle East
and the ruthless borders of enlightened Europe.
All I care about is who to slaughter
in my solipsistic bed tonight.

Texting the Teenage Self

your mother called
you a slut:
>Sexually transmitted distrust
>Lust, and never love
>Urban because you're caged in the steely structure of cities
>Tame which U weren't but wish U had been

and T for terrible trouble tomb tarnish
and T for take which you do
and taken which you are
but truth is T is for trapped
because that's the only state you felt when you
were called a slut by your
Mum, your siblings, your dates
even your cakes. When you opened your mouth to gulp
them, they flashed their teeth
and called you a
>Sexpest
>Loveless
>Umbilical
>Taboo

tolerated only by dark chocolate, not even cakes
by muddy tea, expired milk, rotten cheese
U eat and spit and swallow and escape
and cover your ears but can still hear what
U are

>S.L.U.T.

>Salute to you to your evergreen lust, and your blood
>Loss and blood clots in your breakfast
>U can do better, you could have committed
>   and performed and you could have digested instead of

swallow like an arrowed sparrow, you run and
Take take take and you could not explain to your mother or
to yourself that there was a ray, an energy in their flashing flesh
and glittery eyes that made you grant them what they requested
so you flew from the city of your virginity to a garden infested with flowers
you stared picked sniffed until you were a peacock not a teenage stench
and it is true U are not
tame, and that's O.K. and thou shalt not be taken.

The Cruelty of Impatience

waiting for my girlfriend to come to me
waiting for my girlfriend to come for me
waiting for my girlfriend to laugh at me – so I can weep
waiting for my test results to rescue me
waiting for my boyfriend to put on his lipstick and suck me
waiting for my boyfriend to don his dress and leave
waiting for my country to let me exist
waiting for any country to let me exist
waiting for my employers to pay me
waiting for socialism to breathe
waiting for my wounds to heal
waiting for my relatives to ignore me
waiting for my parents to spoil me
waiting for my siblings to admit
waiting for my friends to vanish – so I can write an award-winning elegy
waiting for my lovers to tell me I'm their one and only as I leave
waiting for my favourite writers to read me
waiting for my favourite writers to ravish me
waiting for my publishers to prioritise me
waiting for my critics to patronise me
waiting for my words to transcend mediocrity

waiting

for the rain to drown me
for the storm to assault me
for spring to come clean
for the moon to bleed
for the autumn to revive me
for the trees to fall on me
waiting for myself to

reach me.

I Am Ash on Wednesdays

Maybe it's Eliot's fault:
all Wednesdays feel ashy to me now.
Feel ashy? More like
a bucket of ash – my mother's and my desires
poured over my head, my eyes
become tears. The ashes itch and blind
me. I see ash, feel ash, breathe ash
everywhere I look has been tarnished
by ash. But what am I claiming?
I cannot look
I cannot see
I am blinded by
ash. Soft grey, detrimental
to my health.
I try to vociferate as
ash fills my mouth and I
fight to breathe.
Fight? Another lie.
Why do I pretend to be strong when
all it takes to translate me to flames
is just a word. A dart-shaped word.
Why do people plan so hard to harass me when
I am made of porcelain; all it takes
is for a breeze to push me and
I fall from my comfortable table and
shatter. Never to be mended.
Shards of sharp ceramic mixed with soft ash
my kohl black blood is a stream of bullets raining
from the ash sky of Wednesdays.
Ash Wednesday?
Did he mean the religious matter?
I do not care. I listen to him bleed and I

let the sense of doom and despair swallow me
for there is nothing again and
it dawns on me that I do not desire
to exist on Wednesdays.

Euston Station

If you're not too unfortunate, false accusations don't land you in jail; they only break your back. You stare at your own voice but can't hear. Everything is too loud. Everything explodes your wound like sirens in spring. Like Euston Station at midnight when you caught three white officers interrogating a Black boy. He was staring into space as if the police didn't exist, as if it was just him and the moon, his skin merging with the night. And you feel black with your back bent, decked with a sable bruise. You hold on to your books and nourish your bruise like it's your child, or that boy. Your bruise an ocean, and when it opens its mouth, you let it devour you, you hope it can drown you. It never does. It spits you back into your white room, snickering, just a false accusation. Why is your back bent? Why are your eyes red? Why do you care? False accusations come and go like period blood. That Black boy is probably free now – like you are.

But if you could face the police one more time, you would open your ashen mouth uttering that you could just tell he was also falsely accused by something more sinister than his skin colour. That you had no evidence, no corroboration, and you didn't even know why he was arrested but you could taste his innocence and it was bitter like yours. But you whirl and turn in the gym mirror, getting fitter, supposedly stronger, and everyone says they're glad you got well and you hope you can turn into steel, with a metallic touch like a second-rate Midas, because by now you know steel is better than gold for it shines less and is more resilient, but there is no steel, no gold, and the black bruise on your broken back gazes out like that boy shouting.

Cliff Trip

Our trip ends when our screams turn
to silence. The silence a precipice from which I fall
as she grabs my hand halfway and I
mumble, *Our time together is jewel.*

She snickers. She wants to share it with all the rats
she collects in her wooden aquarium
and when I tell her I am allergic to rats and
addicted to cats, she shuts me up by calling me a snob.

Our tears fall indistinguishable in the rain over the
precipice. I attempt to breathe while falling
but her ruthless rats attack sucking my little blood
I am not falling; I fell off this cliff a long time ago.

She stares at me, her eyes dark like fire
and she states my selfishness is killing
our love. I stay silent, knowing my selfishness
is the only thing that has kept me alive.

Ritual

Another fucking Sunday when
there is no fuck but endless
arguments about unfucked fuckers.

Another Sunday when I bathe in a white
well and pretend that I'm clean,
so clean I'm almost chaste like a fat virgin.

So clean I lick my skin in search of a floral
scent that would make me dizzy.
Another Sunday when I stifle yet another scream.

Even my white noise is onyx
I am dripping with words and this
makes me a bitch. I wear my shrieks

like a dagger under my garments
I tease my skin with the blade and
slumber. But the Sunday chamber is

the loudest place to sleep in
I wake up, and my sweat smells like
pickled aubergine so strong that the

neighbours call the police. But there is
always featherless hope, a way out, the path
to obsidian peace. If I take out

the blade from underneath my skin
if I find a cobalt vein, and cut it deep,
if my black blood pours out

like acid rain in spring,
these Sundays will end, and
there will be peace.

Blood Days

Break all our delicate cups, my love.
Shatter their bleeding flowers like you
shattered us. I don't mind; because I was
that bad kid, the best student at the back of the class
sleeplessly studying for all
the exams, writing the right
replies to those wrong questions, and yet
cheating just to make sure that all my responses
were conspicuously correct. That I'd get the best grade to
appease my distressed self and expectant parents.
And of course, the addictive thrill of cheating:
the drumming heartbeat, the slippery fingers, the sweaty pen.
A forbidden book open, under the desk, on my trembling lap,
or inked solutions on toilet paper stealing from my grey sleeves.

A retired magician making ends meet in a red circus
ten magicians chewing raw meat, blood oozing
through their teeth.
Ten thousand magicians murmuring your name, a
visceral curse in my scorching ears.

Break everything you please
just beware that loving and hurting you were the
last things I wanted to do, like those cheating days,
a treacherous teenager, trapped, in my dark school.

Bad News

Mother, today your strong hands look wrinkled
and you don't remember my name.
How can you tell me
where you hid the weapons?

Mother, I'm afraid I have some bad news for you
 – as always:
I killed someone today
out of pure pleasure.

Mother, tell me, where are we going now?
Take me somewhere else and tell me if
we lost our Syrian friends to chemical weapons
or bad luck?

Or are we fortunate?
After all, we weren't bombed
and sometimes we drink Christ's blood
in our sunny basements.

Mother, where are we now?
Where are you? And where am I?
Do you still cover your hair with a floral scarf?
Do you still pray to God?

Mother, what are we doing? Are we making stew and rice
for the poor so we won't feel guilty afterwards?
Or have we become poor ourselves? Stoned and sanctioned
and isolated like guinea pigs?

Mother, should I stop whining? And consider us lucky
that we don't have as many honour killings
as Arabs and Pakis? But I can't feel fortunate
I feel bad for them, for every one of us.

Mother, tell me why we should abhor Arabs?
Are we really better than they are? Please, tell me we are.
We have Persian poetry, Persian carpets, and Persian cats.
All they have is oil, Islam, and America.

And yet I confess sometimes, surreptitiously,
I read Mahmoud Darwish and cry.
Mother, let's face it I am one of those weak fighters,
destined to fail.

A country could never be proud of me, I could only be a spy
Nobody needs me and I don't need anybody
I don't need any country
I am free and strong. I don't belong

Mother, I fancy suicide too often, too much.
It makes me calm.
I cannot care that suicide is a sin
I want to go to hell and violate all my friends.

Mother. Please, don't be ashamed that our government
is supporting Assad. My therapist convinced me I
should not be ashamed of the things that aren't my fault,
and according to him nothing has ever been my fault.

Mother, tell me the truth for once. Have you sold
our weapons to feed the poor and buy black scarves?

Mother, why do you act like a prophet?
Like a victorious warrior?
Why don't you accept we have lost the war?
'Which war?' You ask, as if you had no idea

Mother, don't act. Not for me.
'Iraq?' You ask as if you were ignorant, innocent, and young.
'No, not that one, they were as weak as us.'
The Other war.

'Elaborate.' You say like a sadistic teacher.
'The war against everything and everyone.'
Yes, mother, there was a war.
And we lost because we were right.

Mother, I confess I'm not impressed with your strength.
My therapist implied I should not be so power-obsessed
and I'm trying to be cured by his false interpretations because
I like his throat. I meant to only tell you about his neck, but–

Mother, is America going to attack us?
Did you hear their new speech?
But maybe they have a right to loathe us
Our government threatened them first.

Do you think I'm crazy?

When I asked this question of my therapist
whilst staring into his sorry eyes, he took my hands
and squeezed them with an ideal pressure,
a white slave with a fetish for dark hair.

Then I informed him I did not need therapy
and I never did. 'I need your neck.'
I finally showered him with the truth he was after
'I need power.' I guided him to my bed.

Mother, I know it does not make you proud of me
but I swear to you, my only prophet, it was OK
he was sweet in bed and out of bed
until I opened my closet and showed him our weapons.

I need to protect our weapons. Mother, I want to protect your sacred wrinkles,
and like Antigone, I want to bury the corpses of our Syrian friends.
Mother, living people bore me. Shaky like a pot of jelly
afraid to say if they prefer tea or coffee.

Do they fight like us? Do they care about Syria?
Mother, I have news for you: I have stopped caring about Syria, too.

Mother, these days, I don't talk. Nobody really talks. Except about the weather
and the importance of milk in their tea,
grilled sausages and cheese and how well singers can sing.
But mother, let me tell you a secret: singers are the only people who can't sing.

Mother, yesterday I drew a mosque. Then I threw it away as I got scared.
I will not say what I thought. This morning, I drew my therapist and
masturbated on his picture; it was nice. My drawing was nice.
My masturbation was nice. Everything was nice.

I recalled the way I shot him with one of our guns
his blood – the colour of my nail varnish: blue and calm
on my pink, floral sheets. I licked it - it tasted raw.
It tasted like Syria.

Mother, do you think the police will find me?
Do we have enough weapons? And enough time to die?
Mother, I feel safe. His corpse is safe. The world is a safe place.
I'm a good person, like you always asked me to be.

Mother, I don't murder for pleasure, I have morals,
I use clean guns, and I sympathise with the poor.
Mother, I'm a pacifist, can't you see? Coming from the Middle East,
I'm advocating peace; aren't you proud of me?

This Is A Painting Called Motherhood

In the park, glittered by sunlight
   Women pushing prams seem pissed off
(piss dried on the sweaty surface of public toilets)

  Women riding their bikes

                                       Smile
                                       into the sun.

Sunlit Suicide in the Bathtub

After Forough Farrokhzad

All I want is a sunlit suicide in the bathtub, because
I am sick. My intensity is my only friend and my enemy.
Like Mother, who murdered me.
Can you make tea and step on me?
There are thoughts stuck in my throat that won't let me breathe,
and Mother insists I'm obsessed with sinning.
Did you make tea? Can we sin already?
Do you still fancy me: naked, shivering on a rainy beach?
Will you tell my mother that sinning is nothing to me?
That to me, the concept of sin is as expired as that rancid carcass in her fridge?
Ask her to stop discussing politics with me.
Inform her that I'm more interested in counting numbers that don't exist.
Don't make tea, just leave me.
Why is my intensity stuck to me?
Like chewed gum on a dry rock
Like screams on Mother
like grief on Family
like my sins on your flesh
like my thoughts on my throat.
My intensity makes me bleed but my blood is not horrific.
My blood is white like cum as innocent as your throat.
Would you like some?
Where is my tea? In your dirty mug?
I have been stuck in this bathtub for years now, but I still feel unclean
I think I might be sick; it could be the tea, the weak English tea
that's made me sick.
But I admit I've always been sick.
I've always liked to listen to insects have sex.
I want to plunge my nails in the garden of your neck.
I want you to embrace me like a bathtub in spring.
I am sick. I like to repeat something until my teeth break,
the paler your neck, the darker my lips,

the water in this tub is either too hot or too cold, which
makes me want to drown something... or someone.
Can you feel my explosions? My head throbs, an open wound in
whose blood I swim. My sins are a storm, and they've made me
sick; I still relish the sight of your skin, but
turn off the sun please, life under water is serene.
I escape and hospitalise myself in my room underneath my bed,
the heater is exploding but I am
still shivering under my many duvets. I can hear Mother scream.
This was meant to be our empire
instead it's a dead end of wars, a murder scene.
This is when our mothers emerge in our nightmares
informing us that all empires end
in blood, rage, and murdered glory.
That all empires die before they begin.

Smoke Sky

The sky is so tight I want to puncture it with my eyes.
All the boys I wanted
turned up in my mother's funeral
bored and drugged, and no this did not
make them hot
nor did they make me cum.
Every woman I've ever loved plunged
her pens deep inside my smoked-out lungs
and sucked my blood
raw, and no
it was not hot.
I have war fatigue but my frustrations make me strong.
I scoot around this ghost town too pissed off to be suicidal,
been there and done that, selfish and selfless,
I smirk and the sky is sable-black
like my mind.
I bathe in my dirt and urine and count the stars I have
fucked. I am filled with filth and this knowledge
makes me a nervous saint.

RAGESONG

Sister! We are dripping with rage
a diamond in the shape of a tongue
it blinds, gives life, so sharp it cuts,
our rage so glam it's hypno   tic, a violent twitch, a stunning bitch, she
glows in the dark, radiates out of our eyes, she
stalks all the wrongs, the righteous wrongs.
Sister, how much longer will we carry this burden of diamonds, jewels
that pour & poison. I am sick of this constant radiance that feels
    like radiation
we use the sharp edges of our tongues to cut the veins of our fathers, but
when will it end? I know myself; I will always trade my jewels for blood,
    silk for knives
when I say yes, I mean shame, when I say no, I mean emerald gold
Sister, it's always the fathers   the fathers' fathers   oh how we want them
dead & alive   & yes   we
will always say yes as we
                                         shred

their magnifi   cent
                                         flesh

A Manifesto:
The Future Is Queer

Our house has been vandalised again
they have destroyed our bedroom
our bed while we were away falling more deeply in
impermissible love.
They have violated our oceanic space, reduced it to a lake
only to pollute its lucidity, to poison our goldfish
They have violated our love, called it names, accused it of deceit, inauthenticity.
Because we did not conform; their compulsory heterosexuality pins
them down to their comfortable death beds, yet they rise, from their cold coffins
We laugh at their heteronormativity
They detect the scent of laughter on our lovesucked breaths;
It makes them berserk

They call our survivalist pride, vanity,
our subversive intelligence, snobbery,
and our rightful sexuality, abnormality,
our myth-like love, an uncomfortable lie.
They rain and shame, smash and shatter but
we do not utter anything but poetry
they get agitated when we don't look scared
when we gaze back at their violence with our proud faces.

Be patient, my love,
the fire of us will escape from
this dungeon and explode their hollow buildings.
Be patient and behold:

Watch us burn.

ACKNOWLEDGEMENTS

Bad News, Infected Parrot, Game, Sometimes Our Persona Melts in the Sun, and *Sunlit Suicide in the Bathtub* were first published in *Sorrows of the Sun* (Skyscraper Publications, 2017).
Hologram was first published in New Art Projects, February 2018.
I Am Ash on Wednesdays was first published in MIROnline, January 2019.
Made Up was first published in Spontaneous Poetics, February 2019.
An early draft of this book titled *The Rocksong of Sogolsur* was longlisted by the Live Canon pamphlet competition, June 2019.
Blood Days was first published in Ink Sweat & Tears, July 2019.
Eye of the Storm was first published in Harana, October 2019.
The Wicked Capital was first published by Dunlin Press in an anthology called PORT, November 2019.
Dream was first published by New River Press in a booklet called Poetry Against Homelessness, February 2020.
A Manifesto: The Future Is Queer was first published in an anthology Witches, Warriors, Workers: An Anthology of Working Women's Poetry by Culture Matters, March 2020.
Ode to Self was first published in Signal House Edition, July 2020.
Euston Station was first published in Signal House Edition, July 2020.
A Peacock Is A Poem was first published in The Aubrey Beardsley Society, July 2020.
Smoke Sky was first published in Spontaneous Poetics, August 2020.
Sculptures, My Mother Is My Lover, and *introvert schizo is a #mood or Cheap Plastic Thoughts* were first published in SELFFUCK, September 2020.
Cut-up Boy was first published in SCAB, March 2021.
Hiraeth and *In Your Arms I Am A Boy* were first published in The Bombay Review, March 2021.

I wouldn't have composed this Rocksong without the inspiration and assistance of Sheida Mousavi, Stuart Bartholomew, Fran Lock, Nikzad, Keith Jarrett, Dennis Cooper, Sasha Dovzhyk, Jonathan Kemp, Richard Scott, Matt Bates, and my beloved Julia Bell who inspires all my lovesongs.

ABOUT VERVE POETRY PRESS

Verve Poetry Press is a quite new and already award-winning press that focused initially on meeting a local need in Birmingham - a need for the vibrant poetry scene here in Brum to find a way to present itself to the poetry world via publication. Co-founded by Stuart Bartholomew and Amerah Saleh, it now publishes poets from all corners of the UK - poets that speak to the city's varied and energetic qualities and will contribute to its many poetic stories.

Added to this is a colourful pamphlet series, many featuring poets who have performed at our sister festival - and a poetry show series which captures the magic of longer poetry performance pieces by festival alumni such as Polarbear, Matt Abbott and Genevieve Carver.

The press has been voted Most Innovative Publisher at the Saboteur Awards, and has won the Publisher's Award for Poetry Pamphlets at the Michael Marks Awards.

Like the festival, we strive to think about poetry in inclusive ways and embrace the multiplicity of approaches towards this glorious art.

www.vervepoetrypress.com
@VervePoetryPres
mail@vervepoetrypress.com